A guide to
The Wheel of the Year

Discover the fascinating history of the wheel & its festivals

Sasha Jackson

A guide to the wheel of the year
First edition

© 2023 Sasha Jackson / Dartmoor Kin

All rights reserved. No part of this book may be reproduced in any form without permission in writing from the author.

Sasha Jackson

Contents

The wheel of the year 4

   Imbolc 6

   Ostara 8

   Beltane 10

   Litha 12

   Lammas 14

   Mabon 16

   Samhain 18

   Yule 20

      Wheel of the year posters and calendars 23

The wheel of the year calendar (also called a sabbat or pagan calendar) represents the cycle of life and the Earth's seasonal journey around the sun. It follows 8 phases and each one is celebrated by a festival. These represent equinoxes, solstices, and cross-quarter days on the calendar. The wheel of the year is a relatively recent concept, the name was coined along with the festival names, in the 1960's and 70's - to bring together the cycle of events that were so important to, and celebrated by, our ancestors in the northern hemisphere.

Four solar festivals (lesser sabbats) celebrate the winter & summer solstice (*Yule & Litha*), and the spring & autumn equinox (*Ostara & Mabon*). These festivals have been celebrated in many cultures around the world. They are all based on the position of the sun throughout the year; the longest & shortest nights and the 2 occasions when night & day are most equal. The dates of the equinoxes and solstices aren't fixed due to the Earth's elliptical orbit of the Sun - therefore some festivals have a date range, rather than one fixed day.

The four earth festivals (greater sabbats) or cross-quarter fire festivals on the wheel are: *Imbolc, Beltane, Lammas and Samhain.* Traditionally linked to the Anglo-Saxon and Celtic agricultural calendars, they were very important to our ancestors. They mark events like planting and harvesting and are tied to the northern hemisphere's seasons.

Cross-quarter festivals fall 'more or less' midway between the equinoxes and solstices. We traditionally have *fixed* days for these (like Samhain on 31st October) - but some pagans celebrate the *astrological* dates for these festivals instead. As for which you use - fixed or astrological, that depends entirely on the individual, whatever traditions you follow, or simply what appeals to you personally and spiritually. I have added the astrological timing to each festival for reference.

You will find discrepancies between the fixed dates. For example, one person may say that Lammas is on 1st August, but others will say it is the 2nd. This is because for the Celts the start of a new day began at sunset - so the sunset of 1st August to the sunset of 2nd August would be a day in the Celtic calendar - and therefore celebrated through both these dates.

The wheel's 8 festivals honour the practises of our Western European ancestors (mainly Germanic & Celtic). Many of us today find ourselves looking to their old ways, traditions, and beliefs - seeking a connection to (and respect for) our earth that has unfortunately been lost in modern times.

4

The 'Wheel of the Year' that we use today is mainly attributed to modern paganism - where did this term come from? When Christianity spread, the cultures and beliefs of Western European societies (like Celtic, Anglo-Saxon and Germanic) became classified as 'pagan'.

The word *pagan* comes from the Latin word 'pāgānus', meaning 'rural' or 'civilian', and came to mean a worshipper of false gods. The term referred to people who followed a *polytheistic* religion (believing in multiple gods) - the ancient Romans and Greeks for example. The negative association around paganism stems from the world's major *monotheistic* religions (believing in one god). The term was used for anyone who wasn't a member of a monotheistic religion like Christianity. It was an insulting term for what they considered to be an uncivilised person. Sadly, there is still much prejudice and misunderstanding around paganism and what it involves today. Inaccurate, dreadful, and often ridiculous depictions of paganism in television and movies for example – hasn't helped this misconception.

Most of our ancient festivals were phased out as Christianity spread across Europe in the 6th century. The most quoted date for the arrival of Christianity in Britain (though it had been introduced in the British Isles far earlier), is when Saint Augustine arrived in 597 AD on a mission to convert the Anglo-Saxons. The Christian church of course recognized that people were reluctant to give up all of their celebrations - so these were eventually incorporated into the holidays we know today (e.g. Yule = Christmas, Imbolc = Candlemas, Ostara = Easter, Samhain = All Saints' Day).

The modern 'umbrella' of paganism, or neopaganism, encompasses many paths - for example Wicca, Druidry and Heathenry. All these spiritual paths base their beliefs on pre-Christian culture and religion and share a deep respect for nature and the earth. Paganism tries to restore the practices of our Western European ancestors.

Learning about these ancestors is historically fascinating and helps connect us with nature. The origins of these beliefs can be traced back as early as the Palaeolithic people; their art is believed to show early spirituality and understanding of the lunar cycle. 30,000-year-old cave paintings show animal/human figures thought to represent a hunter god and a fertility goddess.

For each festival on the wheel, I've listed some associated colours, objects (to use for an altar or display) and ideas for some family friendly activities.

There is also a 'tree' for each festival - trees tie strongly to pagan history and mythology, and I like their inclusion here. The Celtic Druids had a deep connection to trees, they designated a tree to each of their 13 lunar months and had a 'tree astrology'. To most of our ancient ancestors, all things in the natural world represented the connection with life, the gods, and the earth.

February can certainly feel like a time to hibernate away and wait for spring. It's a dark, cold and short little month - so short that it can pass by without a full moon (dark indeed!). Life is returning though; nature is waking up and signs of growth are emerging everywhere. Many festivals around this month are based on fasting (Christian Lent for example) and purifying for good reason. The word purification comes from the Latin 'februum' and is where February gets its name. This ancient time of cleansing is probably also where 'spring cleaning' comes from! The Anglo-Saxon name for February was Solmonath, meaning 'month of cakes' - cakes and bread were offered to their gods (yum!).

Imbolc *1st to 2nd February / astrological timing: Sun at 15° Aquarius*

Imbolc is a festival that celebrates the awakening of nature and is an important date in the agricultural calendar. It's a quietly powerful time, new life is beginning to emerge after the winter, spring is coming...

The fixed date is usually celebrated from sundown on February 1st and continuing through the day of February 2nd. *Imbolc* (pronounced imulk) comes from the Celtic word *imbolg* meaning 'in the belly', as so much is hidden away, but busy growing at this time of year. Another name for this day is *Oimelc*, meaning 'milk of ewes' as it was the traditional lambing season in the old world. It is a cross quarter day on the wheel of the year calendar, it marks the halfway point between the winter solstice and the spring equinox. The astrological date is around the 3rd or 4th.

Pagan Imbolc celebrations and Christian Candlemas, they essentially celebrate the same things - cleansing, the return of light and the first stirrings of spring. Imbolc - the carrying of burning torches across the farmland prior to new planting. Candlemas - having candlelight processions. Both rituals signifying hope and the end of winter darkness. Snowdrops and fire are symbols of purity linked to both festivals.

Traditionally a Bridey doll or *Brideog* (pronounced 'Bree-jog') was made, with straw or rushes twisted into the shape of a doll and hung over the door. Brigid crosses were also made now and often hung over children's beds. They also were used to bless seed before planting and were believed to aid conception when tucked under the mattress.

The 1st of February is also St Brigid's day, a woman with 2 identities…

'*Brighid or Brigid*' (pronunciations include 'Breej' 'breet' & 'briggid') from the word *Briganti*, meaning 'the high, or exalted one' is the origin of the name Bridget. She is the Celtic goddess of many things: fertility, poetry, smithcraft, healing, fire, water, and divination. Brigid also held dominion over waterways and wells. Coins or food would be left as offerings at these places, many such locations in Ireland were named in her honour.

And the Christian '*St Brigid*', the patroness saint of Ireland. They share many attributes and it's fair to assume that they are probably one and the same (as so many ancient and Christian days have merged over the centuries).

Imbolc associations / display ideas / activities

~ rejuvenation ~ new beginnings ~ creation ~ possibility ~ hope ~ illumination ~

Tree: Rowan - Also known as the 'quickening tree', protects and wards off evil. A rowan twig cross bound with red thread used to be carried or put near the front door. They were often planted in the corner of a farmer's field, to protect their animals and land. Norsemen were known to have used rowan branches as rune staves of protection. The seeds were dried and worn as protective beads.

Colours: Red, white, silver, green.

Display: Snowdrops and other early flowers, fire, milk and dairy products, St Brigid's cross, white feathers, Bridey doll, white & green candles, serpents (they are Celtic symbols of power and divinity), red & white ribbons, poetry, healing herbs, gemstone: amethyst.

Activities: Hang up a Bridey doll or make a traditional St Brigid cross (use pliable twigs, straw or pipe cleaners - or try pretzel sticks 'glued' together with melted chocolate for an edible version). Bake a seed cake (poppy, sunflower, pumpkin seeds). Try making your own butter. Light a fire and toast marshmallows. Spring clean the home. Litter pick on a nature walk.

March may begin cold and windy but by its end, spring is definitely here. Hence the phrase "roar in like a lion and (hopefully) roll out like a lamb". Lambs in the fields, buds on the trees, more daylight and spring flowers blooming. The vernal (spring) equinox is when the day and night are of equal length, and light wins its battle over darkness.

March is named after Mars, the Roman god of war and agriculture. Let the farming and battling commence! (Who wants to do either in the freezing cold?). The Anglo-Saxons called March Lentmonat, literally meaning 'lengthening month'. It is also the origin of the word Lent.

Ostara *20th March / astrological timing: Sun at 0° Aries*

The vernal equinox (a day when the sun sits directly over the equator) celebrates the start of spring. The word *equinox* translates as 'equal night' - the spring and autumnal equinoxes are the two days in the year when the hours of darkness and light are almost equal.

Ostara is one of many names for the spring equinox. It's been celebrated by many cultures, for centuries all around the world (Saxon, Roman, Persian, Maya to name a few). It is a time when everything is in perfect balance and equilibrium - dark and light, masculine and feminine.

The name *Ostara* comes from *Eostre*, the Anglo-Saxon goddess of springtime, fertility, and renewal. There has been some debate as to whether the Anglo-Saxons did worship Eostre; the earliest known mention is from the writings of The Venerable Bede. Bede was an Anglo-Saxon monk, scholar & historian. Whatever the truth, the spring equinox would definitely have been honoured, and a god or goddess was assigned to most of our ancestors' festivals.

Eostre is often depicted with the head of a hare. The hare was a sacred and mystical animal to the Celts. Hares have the extraordinary ability to be pregnant and to still conceive at the same time. Combine this with their habit of producing four litters a year, and you can see why they are an obvious symbol for fertility.

"One old tale tells of Eostre finding a wounded bird, late in the winter. She saves its life by transforming it into a hare, the transformation was not complete however. The bird looks like a hare but retains the ability to lay eggs and would leave these eggs as gifts to Eostre"

It was from Eostre that the Christian celebration of *Easter* and its modern-day symbols evolved. Easter is the first Sunday after the full moon that occurs on, or after, the spring equinox. Eostre also gave its name to the hormone *oestrogen*, essential to women's fertility. Eostre was originally honoured in April, during *Eostremonath* (the Anglo-Saxon name for April). The Anglo-Saxons are believed to have held feasts in her honour, celebrating the arrival of spring and the new planting season.

Ostara associations / display ideas / activities

~ balance ~ renewal ~ change ~ growth ~ rebirth ~ planning ~

Tree: Alder - The alder is flourishing at this time on riverbanks, with its roots in the water, they bridge the magical space between heaven and earth. A whistle or pipe made from alder was thought to summon the faery folk or air spirits. A fairy door in an alder tree was believed to be a gateway to the land of faery or the underworld. It's a uniquely waterproof wood; used in the past for plumbing and bridges. The alder is a tree of silent strength and stability - once used to make shields protecting the front line of an army.

Colours: Yellow, purple, green, pink, pastel colours.

Display: Daffodils and other spring flowers, feathers, coloured eggs, seasonal green vegetables, a symbol of 'balance' (e.g. yin/yang, sun/moon, male/female, light/dark), hares, gemstone: moonstone.

Activities: Plant seeds or bulbs (assigning each one a wish or plan for the coming year). Make an Ostara 'tree' (display some twigs/branches and decorate them with ribbons, feathers etc). Eat hot cross buns (they can be seen as 'cross quarter buns'). Spend time outside celebrating all the new life around you, enjoy a first picnic of the year. Start a nature study journal, or a phenology wheel. Decorate eggs. Make a spring basket for your display.

May makes winter a distant memory, summer is on its way. Wildlife and blossoms are everywhere, making celebration irresistible. It's thought that May is named after *Maia*, the Greek goddess of fertility. The Anglo-Saxon name for May is fantastic - it was *Thrimilci* (pronounced three-milky). This was because the cows could be milked 3 times a day, due to the abundance of green grass they ate at this time!

Beltane *1st to 2nd May / astrological timing: Sun at 15° Taurus*

Beltane (also spelt *Beltaine*) is probably the most well-known pagan festival in Britain. *May Day* itself has ancient origins throughout Europe and has merged with Beltane in modern times. The earliest known May celebration is the *Floralia* 'festival of Flora' (the Roman goddess of flowers). Dating from 238 BC and held from 27th April to the 3rd of May. Today we think of flower girls, morris men, hobby horses, maypoles and the green man (found in legends all over the British Isles).

Beltane falls midway between the spring equinox and the summer solstice. It is a cross quarter fire festival celebrating the beginning of summer and the fertility of the coming year. The celebrations sometimes start the evening before, on the last night of April. The astrological date is around the 5th of May.

The word *Beltane* comes from the Celtic god *Bel* meaning 'the bright one', and the Gaelic word *teine* meaning 'fire'. At Beltane, like Samhain, it is said that spirits wander freely and the veil between the worlds is thinner. Also called 'the feast of the good fires'. Long ago farmers would burn herbs on big bonfires and walk their animals in between them - believing it would protect them from illness. People would also jump over the fires to bring purity and fertility.

10

Some celebrate it as the ritual union of the Spring Goddess (the May Queen) and the Oak King (the May King - also known as Jack-In-The-Green or The Green Man). Their marriage is consummated, and together the May Queen and King symbolise the union of Earth and Sky. This marriage has been re-enacted by humans for centuries; couples would go 'a-maying' in the woods, bringing home hawthorn blossoms after their own 'union'.

Beltane associations / display ideas / activities

~ growth ~ protection ~ sowing ~ love ~ union ~ fertility ~

Tree: Willow - The Druids were thought to craft willow sculptures, this gave rise to the legend of the 'Wicker Man'. The willow is a tree of water and moon magic, also known as 'the tree of enchantment'. Associated with healing, growth and sometimes grief. The painkiller *aspirin* is made from salicylic acid, obtained from willow bark.

Colours: White, red, pink, yellow, green.

Display: Flower crown, ribbons, a mini maypole, hawthorn twigs and blossoms, spring flowers, cup or chalice, antlers, fire, gemstone: rose quartz.

Activities: Make a flower crown (a simple daisy chain will do) or flower basket. Decorate a tree with braided paper ribbons. Make a willow wand (traditionally cut from the tree - who you must thank, at full moon). Light a bonfire. Make a 'green man' mask. Bake Beltane cupcakes (add chopped edible flowers and press rose geranium leaves into the tops before baking, peel off when cool to reveal the pattern). Attach ribbons and little jingle bells to hair scrunchies, wear them on your wrists or ankles.

June is officially summer, astronomically, and metrologically. It has the most daylight of any month and nature is bursting with life, growth, and colour. June is named after the Roman goddess of women and childbirth *Juno*. The Anglo-Saxons called it *Sera Monath*, 'dry month'.

Litha *20th or 21st June / astrological timing: Sun at 0° Cancer*

Midsummer, the peak of the solar year. Many cultures have worshipped the power of the sun, and this is a significant annual turning point for our farming ancestors. The days now grow shorter and shorter until Yule. The summer solstice is called *Litha* - the Anglo-Saxon word for midsummer. Bonfires (representing the fullness of the sun) used to be lit on farmland, sacred spots, and the tops of hills across Europe. Early European traditions celebrated Litha by setting large wheels on fire, they were then rolled down a hill into a body of water. The word solstice comes from the Latin *sol* meaning 'sun' and *sistere* 'to stand still'. One Litha ritual acts out the battle between the Oak King and the Holly King...

"*The Oak and Holly Kings are twin brothers and old enemies, but they are not complete without each other. On the Winter Solstice, or Yule in the wheel of the year, the Oak King battles with Holly and defeats him. Oak now can rule the half of the year until summer. At the Summer Solstice, or Litha, the brothers battle again. This time Holly triumphs and rules until the year turns once again towards the light.*"

In alternative versions of the story, this battle takes place at the equinoxes instead. The Oak King is strongest during Midsummer (Litha), regaining power at the spring equinox (Ostara). The Holly King is strongest during Midwinter (Yule), regaining his power at the autumn equinox (Mabon).

Litha associations / display ideas / activities

~ healing ~ cleansing ~ success ~ love ~ abundance ~ energy ~

Tree: Oak - The sacred oak represents strength, courage, and endurance. The Celtic name for oak is *duir* which means 'door', we enter it to go into the waning part of the year. The ancient druids would only meet for rituals where a fine oak tree was present. Oak in Greek is *drys*, we get the words druid and dryad from this. Dryads were originally the spirits of oak trees, but the term now applies to all tree spirits. Celts, Norsemen, Greeks, and Romans all revered this sacred tree - it is deeply embedded in our folklore. Carry an acorn in your pocket for good luck.

Colours: Gold, orange, yellow, red, green.

Display: Candles in 'sun' colours, sunflowers, honey, sun wheel (make your own using 3 or 4 sticks woven with coloured wool or ribbons - Google 'sun wheel craft'), summer fruits and flowers, mead, oak and ivy leaves, gemstone: tiger's eye.

Activities: Spend lots of time outside in the sun, (BBQ, dance, drum, wild swim, camp). Bake with poppy and sunflower seeds (to represent the battle of darkness and light). Make elderflower cordial (the Elder was a sacred tree with its blooms at their peak now). Create a simple garden sundial (use a straight stick pushed into the ground (or pot), with stones marking the hours).

August is a languid time of ripening and reaping. It can be filled with memories of hazy days, outdoor evenings, long sunny holidays and festivals. The colours are beginning to subtly change, fruit and vegetables are ripe for picking - weeds are flourishing too! The Anglo-Saxon name for August was *Weodmonath*, meaning 'weed month'.

Lammas *1st to 2nd August / astrological timing: Sun at 15° Leo*

This is the 'first harvest' and a cross quarter feast day. *Lammas* is pagan and comes from the Anglo-Saxon phrase 'loaf mass'. Also referred to as 'feast of the first fruits', the first grain would be made into a loaf and blessed. It's often called *Lughnasadh* (pronounced 'loo-na-sa') on wheel of the year calendars. Named for the Celtic festival of *Lugh*, the Celtic sun king and god of craftsmanship. The astrological date is around the 7th or 8th.

Celebrating the wheat harvest was marked by feasts, bread baking, and offerings to the harvest spirits. A bountiful harvest would mean wheat for the coming winter.

The cutting of the first grain and the last are especially significant. The first becoming bread and beer for the community, the last sheaf made into a 'corn dolly' or grain mother (a corn 'hag' was sometimes made instead following a bad harvest) - it was then kept in the home until next year's harvest.

14

There are many customs throughout Europe based around the cutting of the cereal crops (corn, wheat, barley, rye, and oats). Old folk songs sing of *John Barleycorn*, the living spirit of the grain. As the corn is cut, John Barleycorn is cut down too, (embodying death and rebirth) to return as ale and whiskey.

This is an ideal time to give thanks for all the abundance and food we have - and to honour our ancestors and their hard work.

Lammas associations / display ideas / activities

~ harvest ~ achievement ~ success ~ transformation ~ celebration ~ gratitude ~

Tree: Holly - Our most important evergreen. To the ancient Druids holly was second only to the oak in its power and spirituality. The ancients used the wood of the holly to make spears, but also in protective magic - sprigs would be hung in the home for good luck. Holly berries were used to predict winter weather, if there were lots of berries on the tree, it meant that it would be a hard winter.

Colours: Green, shades of harvest - gold, orange, red, light brown.

Display: Bread, dried grains, beer, first harvest fruits & vegetables, grapes, sunflowers, harvest symbols (sickle, scythe), straw braid, corn dolly, gemstone: carnelian.

Activities: Bake bread or cakes. Make a corn dolly from corn husks, or harvest spirit dolls from air drying clay. Take lots of popcorn, thread onto string and hang up popcorn garlands. Have your own Lammas feast.

September is a favourite month of mine, the changing greens of summer into the fiery colours of autumn feels so comforting. The Anglo-Saxons called this month *Haligmonath*, meaning 'holy month'. The time to give thanks and offerings for the second harvest and make preparations for the final one at Samhain.

Mabon *22nd or 23rd September/ astrological timing: Sun at 0° Libra*

Celebrating the autumnal equinox or first official day of autumn. This festival was named in more recent times (probably by modern pagans in the 1970's) after *Mabon*, from Welsh mythology, but it was no doubt celebrated as a harvest festival in ancient times. Mabon marks the turning of the wheel from the light half of the year to the dark.

This is the second harvest, and like *Ostara*, signifies the balance between light and dark (as the day and night are of equal length). It's a time to bring in the crops and prepare for the colder months ahead.

The word harvest comes from the Old English *haerfest* meaning 'autumn'. The main symbol of Mabon is the 'horn of plenty' or cornucopia. It symbolises the abundance of the harvest and might be seen filled with fruits and vegetables and used in a ritual of gratitude.

Autumn is a perfect time to have a deep clean and clear out - declutter and finish projects, both physically and emotionally. Let go of past 'baggage' and set some new goals. Reflect on new hopes and ideas and nurture them for next spring.

Mabon associations / display ideas / activities

~ balance ~ preparation ~ wisdom ~ healing ~ accomplishment ~ gratitude ~

Tree: Vine - *bramble or grape.* The Druids classified anything with a woody stalk as a tree. The vine is an ancient symbol of both happiness and wrath, with imagery of its leaves and fruits even found on Bronze Age artifacts. Celtic people were more likely to have grown blackberry vines, prolific in the British Isles, rather than grapes in their climate. All parts of brambles have been used throughout the centuries for healing, and the ripe fruits used to make wine.

Colours: Deep reds, brown, bronze, copper, gold, orange, yellow.

Display: Apples, harvest fruits & vegetables, cornucopia, acorns, pinecones, vines (bramble or ivy), rosehips, a symbol of 'balance' (e.g. yin/yang, sun/moon, male/female, light/dark), grapes, wine, cider, wild berries, autumn leaves, antlers, gemstone: citrine.

Activities: Go foraging or visit a 'pick your own' farm. Bake an apple cake. Have your own celebratory feast. Make a gratitude list. Preserve your own harvest - make pickles, chutney & jam. Have an autumn deep clean and declutter.

October with its cosy autumnal glow is here. The countryside is glorious now, a blaze of colour, with falling leaves, ripening berries and nuts. A wonderful time for late afternoon walks, before the chills at the end of the month take hold and the clocks go back. The Anglo-Saxon name for this month was *Winterfylleth* 'winter full moon'. They thought that winter officially began on October's full moon. At the end of the month, it was traditional to begin slaughtering livestock, preserving the meat to last through the winter. The Anglo-Saxon name for November was *Blotmonath* meaning 'blood month' for this very reason.

Samhain *31st October to 1st November / astrological timing: Sun at 15° Scorpio*

For many pagans and wiccans, Samhain is the most important festival on the wheel, their 'new year' celebration, and the start of the wheel of the year. *Samhain* (pronounced "sow-en") comes from the Gaelic 'Samhuin' meaning 'end of summer'. It is the third and final harvesting, with the cattle and last crops having been brought in from the fields. Farmers would use up or mulch perishable produce, and slaughter livestock that they did not intend to feed through the winter. It's a time to clear out the old, to enable new things to grow. Symbolically we too can rid ourselves of all that we no longer need.

It is often described as the night where the veil between the dead and the living is at its thinnest, and because of this many Samhain celebrations focus on honouring the ancestors. At Samhain the dark half of the year begins. Death is followed by rebirth and while this is the end of the old year, it is also the beginning of a new one.

People generally begin celebrating Samhain on the 31st of October and this date has become fixed by tradition. It is a cross-quarter festival, which falls midway between the equinoxes and solstices. Some celebrate the *astrological* Samhain instead, occurring around the 7th or 8th of November.

Originally known as the 'feast of the dead', Samhain was celebrated in Celtic countries by leaving offerings of food (particularly 'soul cakes') for the 'wandering dead' on altars and doorsteps. Candles were left burning in a window to help guide the spirits of ancestors and loved ones home, and extra chairs and place settings put at the table for them. Bonfires were lit (once called 'bone-fires' as after eating meat, the bones would be thrown into the fire).

The church adopted these celebrations (like so many others) as 'All Hallows' Eve' (what we now know as *Halloween*), and 'All Saints' Day'. Halloween as most know it today is a rich mix of many traditions, both old and new. Some of the newer ones are sadly very commercialised, bearing little resemblance to the original practices of Samhain.

Samhain associations / display ideas / activities

~ rebirth ~ ancestors ~ wisdom ~ composting ~ endings & beginnings ~ renewal ~

Tree: Reed - Though not a tree - like the vines, the Druids still considered it to be one. Reed was revered for its usefulness. Amongst many uses (baskets, whistles, mats, thatch, quills) one is for insulation - vital as winter sets in. It's associated with protection, healing, wisdom (for their use as writing instruments and paper) and death (due to it being made into arrows). Reed was traditionally cut in November (people living in the countryside would have used wheat instead).

Colours: Black, orange, white, bronze, gold.

Display: Pumpkins, skulls (animal ones can look beautiful), cauldron, besom (twig broom), apples, nuts, berries, black candles, pictures of deceased loved ones, divination items such as runes, gemstone: smoky quartz.

Activities: Have a feast with extra places set for departed loved ones. Light a candle for remembering each of them and let them burn to completion. Make your own besom by gathering a large bundle of birch twigs and tying them together - ritually sweep out the old energy, creating space for new. Create your own ancestors' shrine. Make fondant, clay, or salt dough skulls. Visit a cemetery and make grave rubbings.

December has the shortest day and the longest night of the year. The days may be short and cold but take time to appreciate the beauty of the night in winter. Go outside in the dark, look up, the stars are brightest now and wonderful to behold. Long ago people must have wondered if the sun would ever return, hence this month having celebrations of light in many cultures. The longest night is a time of optimism, the days will now start to lengthen, the sun is returning. Today, at least in Britain, it is mostly associated with Christmas. December was *Aerra Geola* - 'the month before Yule' to the Anglo-Saxons.

Yule *21st or 22nd December / astrological timing: Sun at 0° Capricorn*

The winter solstice, or midwinter, has been acknowledged for centuries. The dark is defeated with the end of the longest night and the return of the light is celebrated. Remember the Holly King, god of the waning year? (Read the tale under 'Litha'). He now surrenders his rule to his brother the Oak King, god of the waxing year, until midsummer.

Yule is probably one of the oldest winter celebrations, marking the return of the sun. A 12-day festival celebrated in the northern hemisphere; it begins on the winter solstice. Many Yule practices can be traced back to the Norse people, they called this festival 'Jul'.

Lots of modern Christmas traditions have evolved from pagan 'Yuletide' ones. If you decorate your home with an evergreen tree, holly or candles, feast, and exchange gifts - you are following these ancient midwinter traditions. When Christianity spread throughout the British Isles, Christians adopted aspects of Yule into a celebration of the birth of Christ. The day was officially set as December 25 by Pope Julius I around 350 AD, to align with the pagan holiday.

The Yule log (though in some cultures a whole tree!) was a highlight of the festival, brought into the home and burnt to symbolise the return of the new-born sun. It is an age-old tradition that seems to have regional variations throughout European folklore. The modern chocolate log so enjoyed today, 'bûche de Noël' (traced back to 19th century Paris), is a tasty alternative!

There are some old traditions: the log mustn't be bought; it should be a gift or harvested from your own land. It's decorated with evergreen foliage, doused with ale, wine or cider, then dusted with flour. Once in the hearth it should be lit using a scrap from the previous year's log. The log burns throughout the night, then smoulders for the 12 days of Yule before being put out. The impracticalities of keeping a log burning today, mean many instead make a candle holder out of a log, to encompass the spirit of the original version.

Though modern Christmas trees are often attributed to Prince Albert introducing them in Victorian times, their origins are far older. Pagan families would bring a live evergreen 'Yule tree' into their home, this gave the wood spirits a place to keep warm in the cold winter, and treats hung on the branches were for the spirits to eat.

Evergreens were very important, they symbolised everlasting life in a season of bare, dead plants. Wreaths made from them were an optimistic reminder that the cold and dark would pass.

Also revered were mistletoe and holly - they represent the 'marriage' of dark and light and the rebirth of the sun. Mistletoe's white berries symbolise male semen, holly's red berries feminine blood. The tradition of 'kissing under the mistletoe' has its origins from this symbolic union.

The pagan tradition of wassailing (pronounced 'woss-ayl-ing') evolved into modern day Christmas carolling. Wassailers would go through their fields and orchards, singing and making loud noises, to scare away any spirits that might spoil the growth of the crops. They would put toast, soaked in beer or cider, into the branches of the trees - to thank them for giving fruit. The expression to 'toast' someone with a drink comes from this tradition. It is still practised in some places today, particularly in the cider producing British West Country.

Yule associations / display ideas / activities

~ celebration ~ reflection ~ peace ~ resting ~ new beginnings ~ gratitude ~

Tree: Elder - The elder is deeply ingrained into the folklore of most northern hemisphere countries, with legends passed down to us from the British Isles, Germany, and Scandinavia. It has one of the strongest reputations for faery and witch superstition, and the most magical protection. Its bark, leaves, flowers and berries are all used in herbal medicine to treat many ailments. You should never cut down an elder according to superstition, and you should grow a rowan near your front door and an elder near your back, for the maximum protection.

Colours: Red, green, white, silver, gold.

Display: Yule log, candles, bells, evergreens, mulled wine or cider, cinnamon & cloves, nuts, pinecones, holly & mistletoe (ideally with their berries), gemstone: clear quartz.

Activities: Make an ornamental Yule log: a branch with 3 or 5 holes carefully drilled on top for candles or tealights (make sure the log can sit safely flat), attach decorative elements using a glue gun. Bake a chocolate Yule log. Go on a walk to gather evergreens for decorating your home (be mindful of the trees and if you're allowed to do so). Go 'wassailing', toast trees and crops with mulled cider or apple juice (have a little yourself too!).

On the following pages are posters of the festivals and some wheel of the year calendars for you to display. Carefully cut them out from the book using a craft knife. More of my guides and calendars can also be found as digital downloads for you to print at home.

Visit: www.payhip.com/DartmoorKin

The wheel of the year calendar represents the cycle of life and the Earth's seasonal journey around the sun. It follows 8 phases and each one is celebrated by a festival. It brings together the cycle of events that were so important to, and celebrated by, our ancestors in the northern hemisphere.

Wheel of the Year

Four solar festivals (lesser sabbats) celebrate the winter & summer solstice (Yule & Litha), and the spring & autumn equinox (Ostara & Mabon). These festivals have been celebrated in many cultures around the world. They are all based on the position of the sun throughout the year; the longest & shortest nights and the 2 occasions when night & day are most equal.

~

The four earth festivals (greater sabbats) on the wheel are: Imbolc, Beltane, Lammas and Samhain. Traditionally linked to the Anglo-Saxon and Celtic agricultural calendars, they were very important to our ancestors. They mark events like planting and harvesting and are tied to the northern hemisphere's seasons. These 'cross-quarter' festivals fall midway between the equinoxes and solstices. Most of our ancient festivals were phased out as Christianity spread across Europe in the 6th century. The Christian church incorporated them into the holidays we know today (e.g. Yule = Christmas, Imbolc = Candlemas, Ostara = Easter, Samhain = All Saints' Day).

~

The wheel's 8 festivals honour the practises of our Western European ancestors (mainly Germanic & Celtic). Many of us today find ourselves looking to their old ways, traditions and beliefs - seeking a connection to our earth that has unfortunately been lost in modern times.

Imbolc is a festival that celebrates the awakening of nature and is an important date in the agricultural calendar. It's a quietly powerful time, new life is beginning to emerge after the winter, spring is coming.

Imbolc
1st February

Usually celebrated from sundown on February 1st and continuing through the day of February 2nd. Imbolc (pronounced imulk) comes from the Celtic word imbolg meaning 'in the belly', as so much is hidden away, but busy growing at this time of year.

~

It is a cross quarter day on the wheel of the year calendar, it marks the halfway point between the winter solstice and the spring equinox.
Imbolc celebrates cleansing, the return of light and the first stirrings of spring. It signifies hope and the end of winter darkness. Snowdrops and fire are its symbols of purity.

~

The 1st February is also St Brigid's day, the Celtic goddess of healing, fire and fertility.

display / activities

Snowdrops and other early flowers, fire, milk and dairy products, St Brigid's cross, white feathers, Bridey doll, white & green candles, serpents (they are Celtic symbols of power and divinity), red & white ribbons, poetry, healing herbs, gemstone: amethyst.

~

Hang up a Bridey doll or make a traditional St Brigid cross (use pliable twigs or pipe cleaners - or try pretzel sticks 'glued' together with melted chocolate for an edible version). Bake a seed cake (poppy, sunflower, pumpkin seeds). Make your own butter. Light a fire and toast marshmallows. Spring clean the home. Litter pick on a nature walk.

Ostara is one of many names for the vernal equinox. It's been celebrated by many cultures, for centuries all around the world. It is a time when everything is in perfect balance. It celebrates the start of spring.

Ostara
20th March

The spring and autumnal equinoxes are the two days in the year when the hours of darkness and light are almost equal. The word equinox translates as 'equal night'.

~

The name 'Ostara' comes from 'Eostre', the Anglo-Saxon goddess of springtime, fertility and renewal. She is often depicted with the head of a hare, they were a symbol of fertility and a sacred animal to the Celts.

~

"One old folktale tells of Eostre finding a wounded bird. She saves its life by changing it into a hare, but the transformation wasn't completed, the bird looked like a hare but could still lay eggs - it would leave these as gifts to Eostre".
This is where the Christian celebration of Easter and it's modern day symbols come from.

display / activities

Daffodils and other spring flowers, feathers, coloured eggs, seasonal green vegetables, a symbol of 'balance' (e.g. yin/yang, sun/moon, male/female, light/dark), hares, gemstone: moonstone.

~

Plant seeds or bulbs (assigning each one a wish or plan for the coming year). Make an Ostara 'tree' (display some twigs/branches and decorate them with ribbons, feathers etc). Eat hot cross buns (they can be seen as 'cross quarter buns'). Spend time outside celebrating all the new life around you, enjoy a first picnic of the year. Start a nature study journal, or a phenology wheel. Decorate eggs. Make a spring basket for your display.

Beltane falls midway between the spring equinox and the summer solstice. It marks the beginning of summer and the fertility of the coming year.

Beltane
1st May

One of the most well-known pagan festivals in Britain. May Day has ancient origins throughout Europe and has merged with Beltane in modern times. Today we think of flower girls, morris men, maypoles and the green man (found in legends all over the British Isles). At Beltane, like Samhain, it is said that spirits wander freely and the veil between the worlds is thinner.

~

The word Beltane comes from the Celtic god Bel meaning 'the bright one', and the Gaelic word teine meaning 'fire'. Also called 'the feast of the good fires'. Long ago farmers would burn herbs on big bonfires and walk their animals in between them - believing it would protect them from illness. People would also jump over the fires to bring purity and fertility.

~

Some celebrate it as the ritual union of the Spring Goddess and the Oak King. Their marriage is consummated, and together the May Queen and King symbolise the union of Earth and Sky. This marriage has been re-enacted by humans for centuries; couples would go 'a-maying' in the woods, bringing home hawthorn blossoms after their own 'union'.

display / activities

Flower crown, ribbons, a mini maypole, hawthorn twigs and blossoms, spring flowers, cup or chalice, antlers, fire, gemstone: rose quartz.

~

Make a flower crown (a simple daisy chain will do) or flower basket. Decorate a tree with braided paper ribbons. Make a willow wand (traditionally cut from the tree - who you must thank, at full moon). Light a bonfire. Make a 'green man' mask. Bake Beltane cupcakes (add chopped edible flowers and press rose geranium leaves into the tops before baking, peel off when cool to reveal the pattern). Attach ribbons and little jingle bells to hair scrunchies, wear them on your wrists or ankles.

Midsummer, the peak of the solar year. The summer solstice is called Litha - the Anglo-Saxon word for midsummer.

Litha
20th / 21st June

The word solstice comes from the Latin sol meaning 'sun' and sistere 'to stand still'. Many cultures have worshipped the power of the sun, and this is a significant annual turning point for our farming ancestors. The days now grow shorter and shorter until Yule.

~

Bonfires (representing the fullness of the sun) used to be lit on farmland, sacred spots, and the tops of hills across Europe. Early European traditions celebrated Litha by setting large wheels on fire, they were then rolled down a hill into a body of water.

~

One Litha ritual acts out the battle between the Oak King and the Holly King - "The Oak and Holly Kings are twin brothers and old enemies, but they are not complete without each other. On the Winter Solstice, or Yule, the Oak King battles with Holly and defeats him. Oak now can rule the half of the year until summer. At the Summer Solstice, or Litha, the brothers battle again. This time Holly triumphs and rules until the year turns once again towards the light."

display / activities

Candles in 'sun' colours, sunflowers, honey, sun wheel (make your own using 3 or 4 sticks woven with coloured wool or ribbons), summer fruits and flowers, mead, oak and ivy leaves, gemstone: tiger's eye.

~

Spend lots of time outside in the sun, (BBQ, dance, drum, wild swim, camp). Bake with poppy and sunflower seeds (to represent the battle of darkness and light). Make elderflower cordial (the Elder was a sacred tree with its blooms at their peak now). Create a simple garden sundial (use a straight stick pushed into the ground (or pot), with stones marking the hours).

This is the 'first harvest' and a cross quarter feast day. 'Lammas' is pagan and comes from the Anglo-Saxon phrase 'loaf mass'. Also referred to as 'Lughnasadh' (pronounced 'loo-na-sa') after the Celtic festival of Lugh, the Celtic sun king.

Lammas
1st August

There are many customs throughout Europe based around the cutting of the cereal crops (corn, wheat, barley, rye and oats). Old folk songs sing of John Barleycorn, the living spirit of the grain. As the corn is cut, John Barleycorn is cut down too, (embodying death and rebirth) to return again as ale and whiskey.

~

The cutting of the first grain and the last are especially significant. The first becoming bread and beer for the community, the last sheaf made into a 'corn dolly' or grain mother (a corn 'hag' was sometimes made instead following a bad harvest) - it was then kept in the home until next year's harvest.

~

Celebrating the wheat harvest was marked by feasts, bread baking, and offerings to the harvest spirits. A bountiful harvest would mean wheat for the coming winter. This is an ideal time to give thanks for all the abundance and food we have - and to honour our ancestors and their hard work.

display / activities

Bread, dried grains, beer, first harvest fruits & vegetables, grapes, sunflowers, harvest symbols (sickle, scythe), straw braid, corn dolly, gemstone: carnelian.

~

Bake bread or cakes. Make a corn dolly from corn husks, or harvest spirit dolls from air drying clay. Take lots of popcorn, thread onto string and hang up as garlands. Have your own Lammas feast.

Mabon celebrates the autumnal equinox, the first day of autumn. It's a time to bring in the crops and prepare for the colder months ahead.

Mabon
22nd / 23rd September

This festival was actually named in more recent times (probably by modern pagans in the 1970's) after Mabon, from Welsh mythology. Mabon marks the turning of the wheel from the light half of the year to the dark. This is the second harvest, and like Ostara, signifies the balance between light and dark (as the day and night are of equal length).

~

The word harvest comes from the Old English haerfest meaning 'autumn'. The main symbol of Mabon is the 'horn of plenty' or cornucopia. It symbolises the abundance of the harvest and might be seen filled with fruits and vegetables and used in a ritual of gratitude.

~

Autumn is a perfect time to have a deep clean and clear out - declutter and finish projects, both physically and emotionally. Let go of past 'baggage' and set some new goals. Reflect on new hopes and ideas and nurture them for next spring.

display / activities

Apples, harvest fruits & vegetables, cornucopia, acorns, pinecones, vines (bramble or ivy), rosehips, a symbol of 'balance' (e.g. yin/yang, sun/moon, male/female, light/dark), grapes, wine, cider, wild berries, autumn leaves, antlers, gemstone: citrine.

~

Go foraging or visit a 'pick your own' farm. Bake an apple cake. Have your own celebratory feast. Make a gratitude list. Preserve your own harvest - make pickles, chutney & jam. Have an autumn deep clean and declutter.

For many Samhain is the most important festival on the wheel, the 'new year' celebration, and the start of the wheel of the year. Samhain (pronounced "sow-en") comes from the Gaelic 'Samhuin' meaning 'end of summer'.

Samhain
31st October

Samhain is the third and final harvest. Farmers would use up or mulch perishable produce, and slaughter livestock that they did not intend to feed through the winter. It's a time to clear out the old, to enable new things to grow. Symbolically we too can rid ourselves of all that we no longer need. People generally begin celebrating on the 31st of October and this date has become fixed by tradition. It is a cross-quarter festival, which falls midway between the equinoxes and solstices.

~

Originally known as the 'feast of the dead', Samhain was celebrated in Celtic countries by leaving offerings of food for the 'wandering dead' on altars and doorsteps. It is often described as the night where the veil between the dead and the living is at its thinnest, and because of this many Samhain celebrations focus on honouring the ancestors. Candles were left burning in a window to help guide the spirits of loved ones home, and extra chairs and place settings put at the table for them.

~

The church adopted these celebrations (like so many others) as 'All Hallows' Eve' (what we now know as Halloween), and 'All Saints' Day'. Halloween as most know it today is a rich mix of many traditions.

display / activities

Pumpkins, skulls (animal ones can look beautiful), cauldron, besom (twig broom), apples, nuts, berries, black candles, pictures of deceased loved ones, divination items such as runes, gemstone: smoky quartz.

~

Have a feast with extra places set for departed loved ones. Light a candle for remembering each of them and let them burn to completion. Make your own besom by gathering a large bundle of twigs and tying them together - ritually sweep out the old energy, creating space for new. Create your own ancestors shrine. Make fondant, clay or salt dough skulls. Visit a cemetery and make grave rubbings.

The winter solstice, or midwinter, has been acknowledged for centuries. The dark is defeated with the end of the longest night and the return of the light is celebrated.

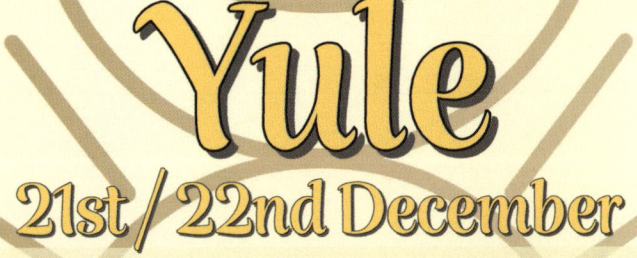

Yule
21st / 22nd December

Yule is probably one of the oldest winter celebrations, marking the return of the sun. Many Yule practices can be traced back to the Norse people, they called this festival 'Jul'. Lots of modern Christmas traditions have evolved from these 'Yuletide' ones. If you decorate your home with an evergreen tree, holly & candles, feast, exchange gifts - you are following these ancient midwinter traditions. Christians adopted Yule into a celebration of the birth of Christ. Pope Julius I set the day in 350 AD, to align with the pagan holiday.

~

The Yule log was a highlight of the festival, brought into the home and burnt to symbolise the return of the new-born sun. It is an age-old tradition with variations throughout European folklore. Families would bring an evergreen 'Yule tree' into their home. Evergreens were very important, they symbolised everlasting life, wreaths made from them were an optimistic reminder that the cold and dark would pass. Also revered were mistletoe and holly - they represent the 'marriage' of dark and light and the rebirth of the sun.

~

The pagan tradition of wassailing (pronounced 'woss-ayl-ing') evolved into modern day Christmas carolling. Wassailers would go through fields and orchards, singing and making loud noises, to scare away spirits that might spoil the growth of the crops.

display / activities

Yule log, candles, bells, evergreens, mulled wine or cider, cinnamon & cloves, nuts, pinecones, holly & mistletoe (ideally with their berries), gemstone: clear quartz.

~

Make an ornamental Yule log: a branch with 3 or 5 holes carefully drilled on top for candles or tealights (make sure the log can sit safely flat), attach decorative elements using a glue gun. Bake a chocolate Yule log. Go 'wassailing', toast trees and crops with mulled cider or apple juice.

Wheel of the Year

- **31 Oct — Samhain** — All Hallows Eve
- **21/22 December — Yule** — Winter Solstice
- **1 February — Imbolc** — New beginnings
- **20 March — Ostara** — Spring Equinox
- **1 May — Beltane** — May Day
- **20/21 June — Litha** — Summer Solstice
- **1 August — Lammas** — Lughnasadh
- **22/23 September — Mabon** — Autumn Equinox

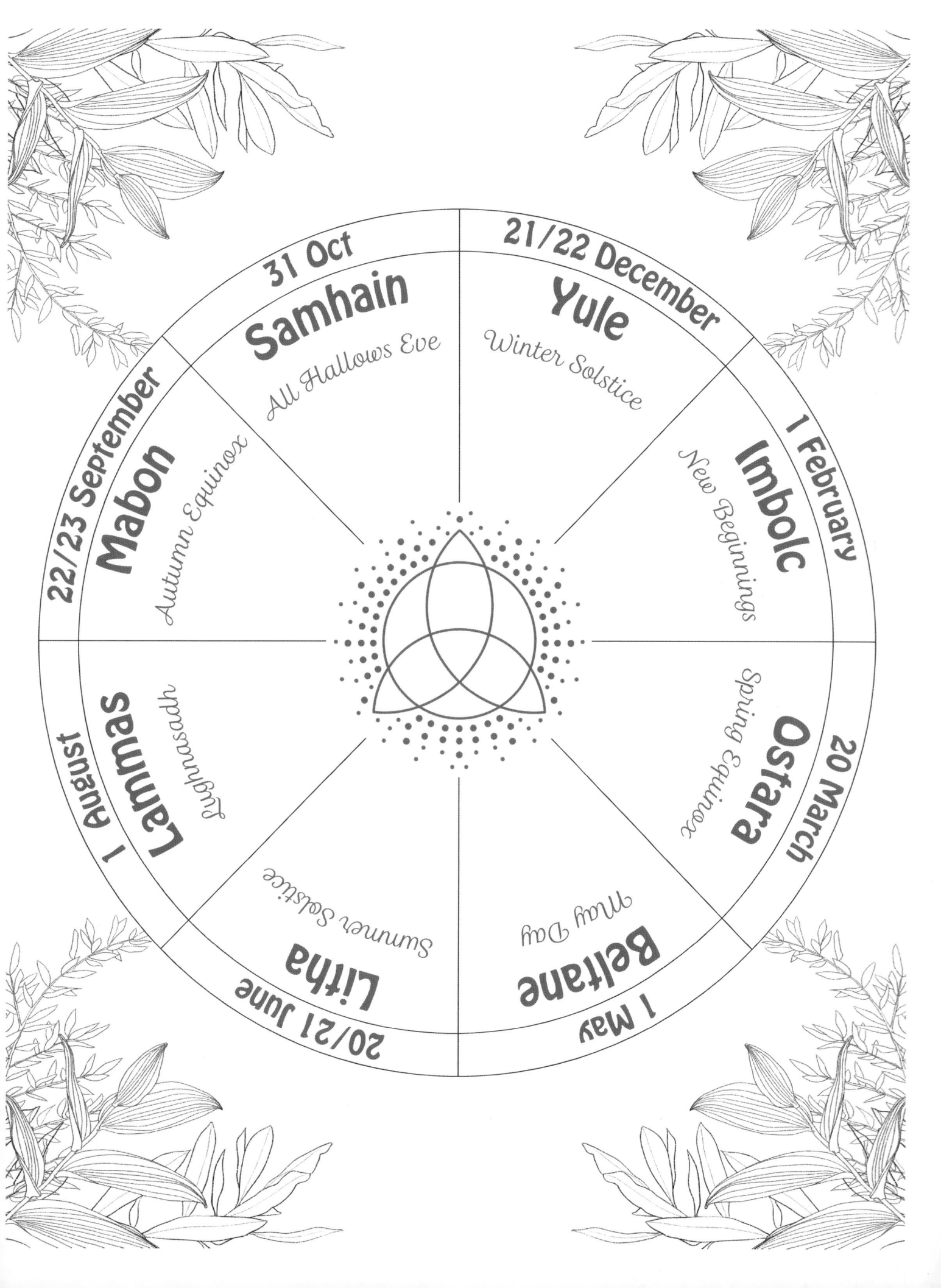

Wheel of the Year

- **Samhain** — 31 Oct — All Hallows Eve
- **Yule** — 21/22 December — Winter Solstice
- **Imbolc** — 1 February — New Beginnings
- **Ostara** — 20 March — Spring Equinox
- **Beltane** — 1 May — May Day
- **Litha** — 20/21 June — Summer Solstice
- **Lammas** — 1 August — Lughnasadh
- **Mabon** — 22/23 September — Autumn Equinox

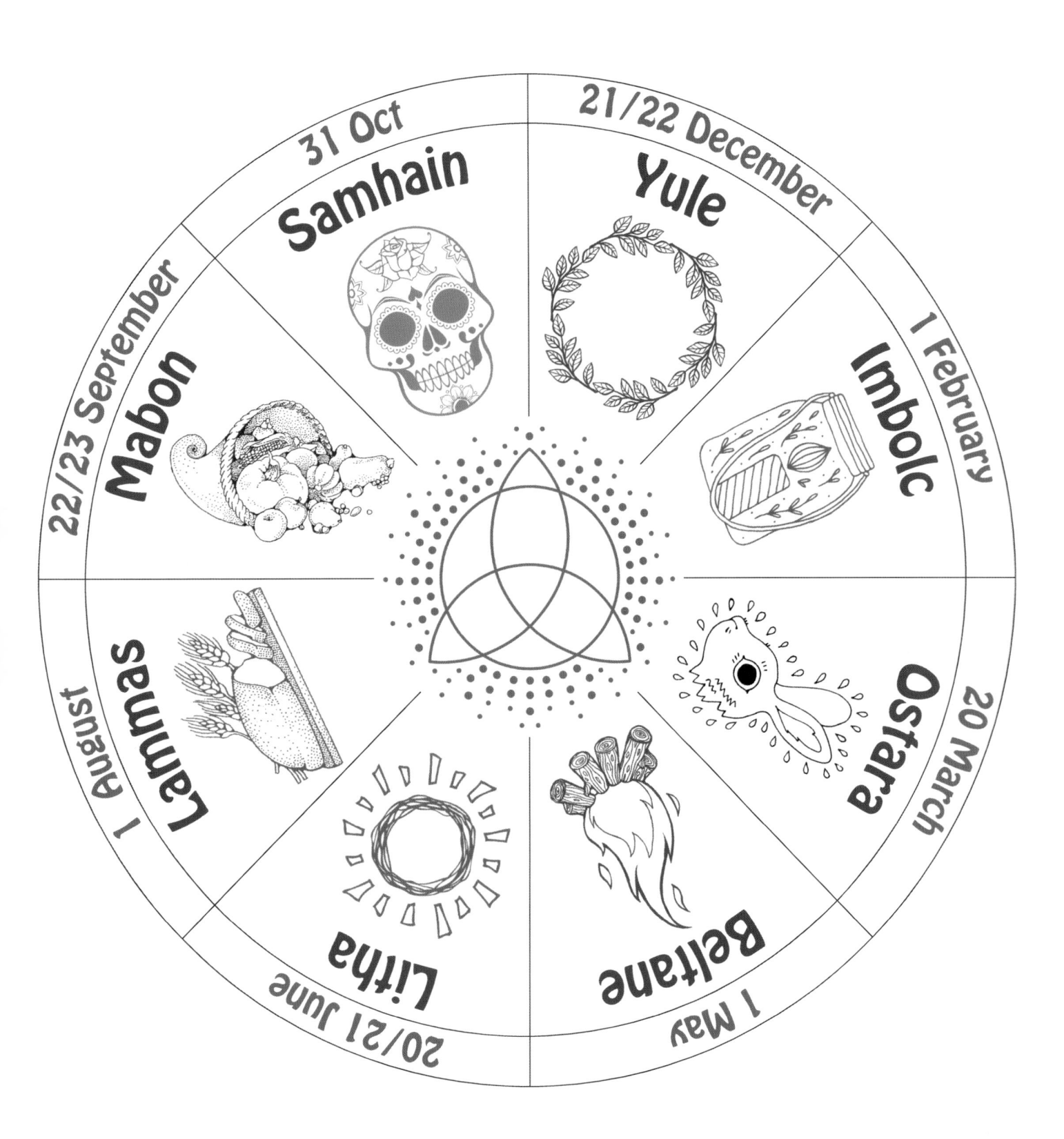

Wheel of the Year

- **Samhain** — 31 Oct
- **Yule** — 21/22 December
- **Imbolc** — 1 February
- **Ostara** — 20 March
- **Beltane** — 1 May
- **Litha** — 20/21 June
- **Lammas** — 1 August
- **Mabon** — 22/23 September

Author bio.

Sasha Jackson - Photographer, digital artist, daydreamer and home educating mum to 3 boys. She spent years learning about the origins of the wheel of the year, whilst studying ancient European history. Under her shop name of 'Dartmoor Kin' Sasha also designs printable digital downloads. Most of her resources are ideal for using with a nature curriculum or journal, with topics like moon phases, wheel of the year calendars, phenology guides and nature study wheels. She lives in a beautiful Devon village on the edge of Dartmoor National Park, England.

Visit: **www.payhip.com/DartmoorKin**
for more guides and downloads.

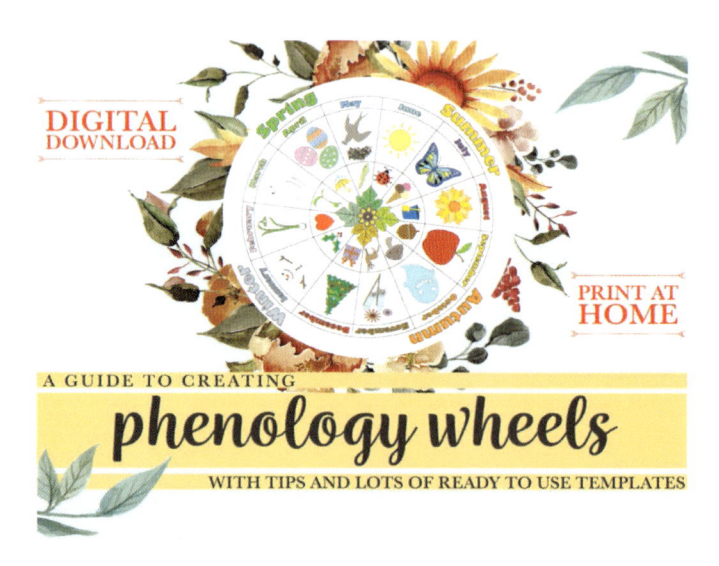

Printed in Great Britain
by Amazon